SUDAN RELIEF AND REHABILITATION ASSOCIATION

HUMAN RIGHTS ABUSES IN THE SUDAN 1987

THE
DHEIN MASSACRE SLAVERY
IN THE SUDAN

BOL GAI DENG

Ordering Information:

For orders and inquiries, please contact:
1-888-404-1388
www.goldtouchpress.com
book.orders@goldtouchpress.com

Printed in the United States of America

CONTENTS

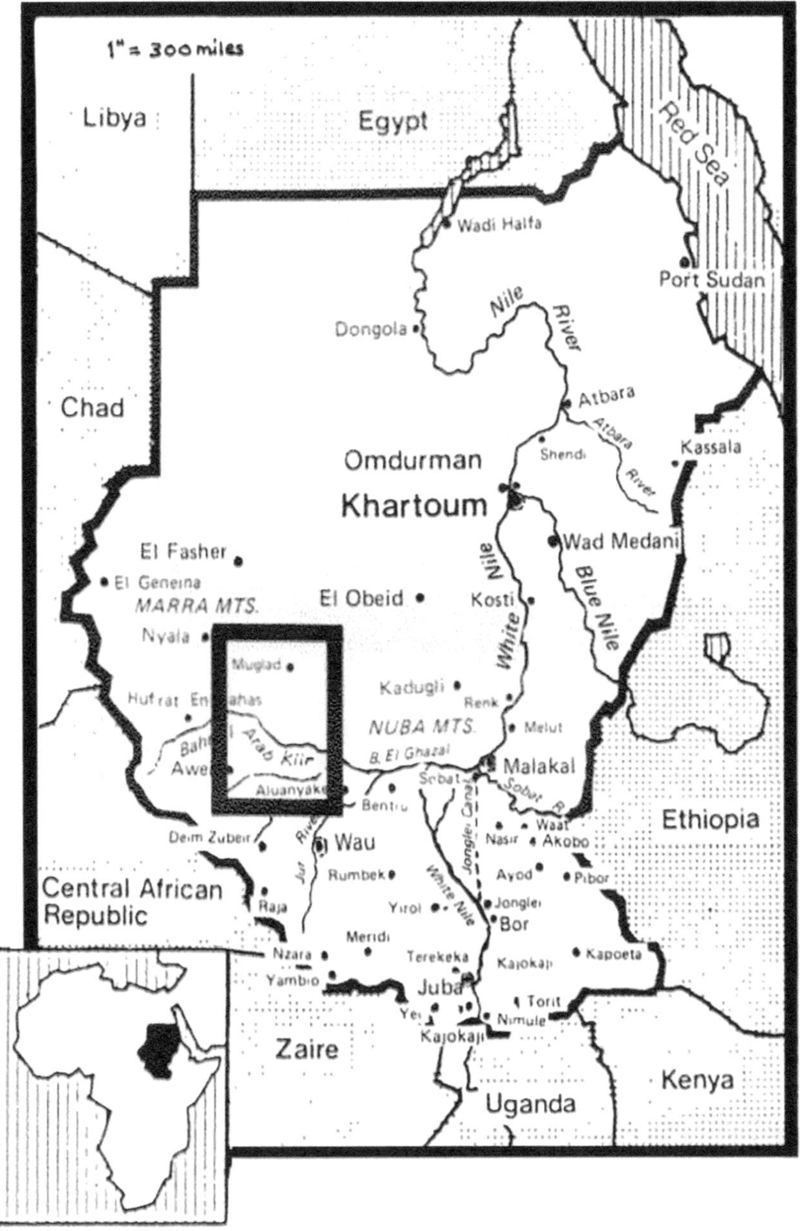

Map 1: The Sudan, showing the area of Bahr al-Arab-Kiir

PREFACE

We believe it is the role of Sudanese intellectuals to squarely address instances of the violation of human rights in the country. And it was this belief which prompted us to investigate the Dhein massacre and the re-emergence of slavery in the Sudan.

We started our .investigations after we had met in Nyala toward the end of May 1987. Dr Suleyman Ali Baldo was on a mission to establish a training centre for homeless children. And Dr Ushari Ahmed Mahmud was conducting research on the language situation in Darfur.

We used to meet and discuss the homeless and local languages. But the Dhein massacre was the main topic of discussion in all circles in Nyala. We were by then aware that serious events had taken place in Dhein, and that the government was attempting a cover-up. However, the various accounts of the massacre in Nyala were contradictory, and the explanations were too superficial for carnage of the magnitude which was mentioned.

We therefore decided to conduct an independent investigation into the massacre and its causes. And this led us to meet with dozens of eyewitness survivors who the development of events to us. But we also came to receive information and evidence about another continuing violation of human rights — slavery.

We present the results of our investigations into the massacre and the practice of slavery in this report. We hope that it will encourage others to work to expose publicly all violations of human rights in the Sudan So that we may work together to change the conditions that make such violations possible.

We register our thanks to the eyewitness survivors whose stories make up the basis for this report. Without their help and their courage in coming forward and giving information, the facts about this massacre would have continued to be shrouded in mystery and eventually lost in oblivion. We provide their full names so that other investigators may corroborate our findings, and to facilitate further research into the massacre and its causation.

We also thank all our colleagues who read and commented on the manuscript. We particularly thank Dr. Khidir Abdel-Karim and Dr. Taysir Mohamed

Ushari Mahmud
Suleyman Baldo
Khartoum, July 1987

INTRODUCTION

This is a report about the massacre which took place in the town of Dhein, in western Sudan. On March 27–28, more than a thousand Dinka children, women and men were killed and burnt to death by some Rizeigat Arabs and others in the town.

This report also includes information about the existence of slavery in Dhein and the surrounding areas.

The objectives of this report are as follows:—

1. To provide information about the massacre to the Sudanese people and the international community.
2. To show the need for immediate assistance for the survivors of the massacre.
3. To show the need for legal assistance for the survivors and the victims' relatives.
4. To call on public opinion, both local and international, to exert pressure and to agitate for the dismantling of the institution of slavery in the Sudan.
5. To analyse the root causes of the massacre, and expose the role of government policy in it.

What prompted us to start investigating the massacre and to prepare this report was the government's attempt at a cover-up, and the Prime Minister's explanation of the massacre as no more than an act of revenge (BBC May 31).

The report is mainly based on the personal testimonies of survivors of the massacre. We visited them in Kas, Nyala, Khartoum, and in Dhein.

In the first chapter, we present a brief description of Dhein town: its location, ethnic composition, the government presence in it, and the situation of the Dinka and the Church.

In the second chapter, we give a detailed description of the events of the massacre. We also include sections dealing with questions such as: the of dead, the identity of the killers, the role of government officials and the behaviour of the police, the fact that the massacre was planned, and the situation of the survivors in the aftermath of the massacre.

Chapter three discusses the root causes of the massacre. It shows that government policy has produced distortions in the Rizeigat community such as banditry and slavery, which interacted with social conflicts in Dhein to generate a massacre psychosis.

Chapter four presents the personal testimonies Of Seven Dinkas affected by the institution of slavery.

Map 2: The Area Of Conflict:
Southern Darfur and northern Bahr el Ghazal Provinces

CHAPTER ONE
THE TOWN OF DHEIN

Location, Inhabitants and Position

Dhein is the main town in the eastern district of southern Darfur Province. It has a population of about 60 thousand people, the majority of whom are from the Rizeigat ethnic group. Other groups include the Dinka, Fur, Zaghawa, Birgid. Barti, and Hausa.

Dhein occupies a central position in the war between the Government and the SPLA to the south of Bahr al–Arab-Kiir. The Government-supported militias have drawn many of their members from the Rezeigat of Dhein, and those in charge of these armed militias procure money for guns and ammunition from several sources, one of which is certain Dhein merchants.

Some of the cattle stolen by the militias, and also some of the kidnapped Dinka women and children. find their way to the town of Dhein.

Dhein is not an isolated place in a remote corner of the Sudan. Rather, it is a town which has links by rail and lorry traffic in many directions. It is also a major commercial centre in Darfur, and a centre for the grain and cattle trade.

Government Presence

The government maintains a conspicuous presence in Dhein, which is the site of the headquarters of the Eastern District Council. This is headed by an Administrative Officer of high rank, named Adam al-Tahir. The town has a civil court with a resident judge, named Wad al-Mubarak. A people's court is manned by some of the top Rizeigat sheikhs, like Ali al-Radi and Hammad Bushara.

There is a police station headed by a colonel who was not present in Dhein during the massacre. His deputy. Ali al-Manna was therefore in charge, assisted by another officer and several policemen. There is also a police unit in charge Of passports and nationality, and another unit at the railway station. There is a prison and a fire department. However, there is no army presence in Dhein.

Dhein has a distinguished location on the political map of the Sudan. It is one of the areas of influence of the Umma Party. One of the top leaders of this Party, Dr. Adam Musa Madibbu, is from Dhein. He is a former university lecturer and currently the Minister of Energy. Dr Madibbu visited Dhein after the massacre at the head of a tact-finding mission. On his return he issued a statement about the 'security situation in the area' and about the formation of a committee' of local authorities, administrators and regular forces to investigate 'the events Of Bahr and Dhein' (SUNA 27/4/1987).

The Dinkas in Dhein

Systematic migration by the Dinkas to Dhein started during the first civil war in 1964. At that time large numbers came and settled there. After the Addis Ababa Peace Accord in 1972, the majority went back to their previous areas south of Bahr al-Arab-Kiir. After the second civil war broke out, and particularly due to repeated attacks on their villages by the Misseiriya and Rizeigat armed militias, thousands of the Dinkas in the area moved into Dhein, among many other locations.

In May 1986, a census of the Dinkas in Dhein was conducted by an Islamic group for the purpose of Islamisation and relief work. The total number, excluding children, was 16, 970.

The economic activities of the Dinka in Dhein included: agricultural labour, work in the bean factories, brick–layers, and house servants. Others worked in temporary jobs like bringing grass for building, house building, extracting water melon seeds, and digging latrines.

Very few Dinkas in Dhein were employed by the government: two policemen, a driver in the Council, a worker in the Water Department, and another worker in the Railway Station. The 37 or so railway workers who were burnt to death in the Police Centre, were from Jur Chol ethnic group.

The Church

The church was built in Dhein around 1964 when numbers of Dinkas migrated to the town. It was given a plot of land by one of the Rizeigat sheikhs. On its part, the church attempted to develop cordial relations with the Muslim community. It started English language classes and a nursery open to all.

However, a degree of hostility and suspicion recently developed against the church. Some 400 Muslims sent a petition to the judge asking for it to be removed. There were other disputes over land, and suspicions about the church's solar energy system and its Sunday 'meetings'.

These were some of the features of Dhein that may help us to contextualise the massacre. In a later section we discuss the social and religious conflicts that were rampant in Dhein before the massacre.

CHAPTER TWO

THE MASSACRE

In this section, we give a detailed description of the massacre which is based on the accounts of eyewitness survivors. They described how they were attacked, the methods of killing and burning, and the weapons used. They also spoke of the rote of government officials and the behaviour of the police during the massacre. Some of them provided information which indicates that the massacre was planned; and that the police were expecting an attack by the Rizeigat Arabs on the Dinkas.

Outline of Events

Before we present the details of the massacre, we give an outline of the events which will enable the reader to follow the details.

The massacre started on the evening of Friday, March 27, 1987. A group of armed Rizeigat attacked the church where 25 Dinkas were congregated after an evening prayer.

This same group, or possibly another one, then attacked the homes of some Dinka families in the neighbourhood. They burned down a number of houses and killed 5 (or 7) Dinkas.

That same Friday night, some Dinkas fled from the town. Some of them hid with Dhein families, and the rest were grouped in Hillat Sikka Hadid, a neighbourhood near the railway station. They were under police protection.

On Saturday morning, government officials moved the Dinkas who had stayed the night in Hillat Sikka Hadid to the railway station. The intention was to take them out of the town for their own protection. The Dinkas were distributed among the different railway wagons. They filled eight of these. The rest stayed in the station police centre.

Then swarms of Dhein inhabitants, the majority of them Rizeigat, moved into the railway station, and started attacking the Dinkas. More than a thousand Dinkas had been killed by sunset on Saturday. The train then moved off carrying the survivors to Nyala.

In the following sections we will present the details of the events of:

1. Friday, March 27, 1987
2. Saturday. March 28, 1987
3. Saturday evening — Sunday morning, March 28–29. 1987

Then we address the following questions: the number of victims, the identity of the murderers, the role and behaviour of the police and government officials, what happened to Reverend Benjamin Kon and the Dinka chiefs, and information that the massacre was planned and anticipated.

The Development of Events
The evening of Friday March 27

The events of Friday evening included: the attack on the church, the burning of Dinka homes in Hillat Fog, the flight of the Dinkas to the police station for protection, moving the Dinkas from the police station to a school yard nearby, and finally moving them again to Hillat Sikka Hadid where they spent the night. During this night 5-7 Dinkas were killed and several fled the town.

1. The attack on the church

The church of Dhein holds daily prayers. But most Christian Dinkas come on Sunday (about 50 people) and on Friday (about 30). Friday is the weekly holiday, and Christian Dinkas come to church for evening prayers that end at about 7pm, after which they sit together in the church to chat.

Every Friday evening, the Youth Society of the neighbourhood where the church is situated, holds a meeting in the open space in front of the church. The majority of the members Of this society are Rizeigat Arab Moslems. They used to have cordial relations with the church. That evening, they did not hold their regular meeting.

On the evening of Friday March 27, the number of people who came to the evening prayers was 32. Twenty-seven stayed on after the prayers.

Without warning, about fifty Rizeigat Arabs attacked them. They were armed with spears, knives, sticks, and a gun. The beat the Dinkas in the church and chased them out. Nobody was killed.

Then the attackers moved on to attack the neighbouring Dinka homes, beating the inhabitants, and burning down some houses.

That was the beginning of the Dhein massacre.

2. The burning of Hillat Fog

Hillat Fog lies in the south-eastern part of the town and is the area where the largest number of Dinkas live. The attackers moved in and started burning down the houses and beating the Dinkas. This time the number of attackers was much greater and included women and young boys.

The attackers obstructed the police and stopped the fire engine from reaching the fires to put them out. Five to seven Dinkas were killed. They included Deng Garang. Makot Aiwel and Thiep Aleu.

After this attack the Dinkas dispersed in different directions. Some fled to the town; others ran to the north-eastern part of the town to Hillat Sikka Hadid where Dinkas live with several other ethnic groups; some hid with families; and many ran to the police station for protection.

3. Refuge in the police station

By about 8pm the police station yard was packed with Dinkas fleeing from the attack of the Rizeigat Arabs. A few policemen stood on guard.

The Administrative Officer, Adam al-Tahir, was there. He is the highest government official in the town and in the Eastern District of Southern Darfur Province. The deputy chief of police, Ali al-Manna, was in charge since his chief was away in Nyala. The officials decided to protect the Dinkas, and waited for a response to the telegrams which they had sent to Nyala.

4. Moving to the primary school

The primary school lies to the west of the police station. Its walls were higher and would offer better protection than the police station with its broken fence, so the government officials decided to move the Dinkas here. However, their stay here was not tong. Again it was decided to move them to Hillat Sikka Hadid.

5. Spending the night in Hillat Sikka Hadid

Hillat Sikka Hadid is a multi ethnic neighbourhood which lies adjacent to the railway station. About a thousand Dinkas live here. Now thousands more came seeking protection. Some came directly following the attack on Hitlat Fog. Now, those who were in the police station and then in the school yard were also moved here.

That night, some merchants of Dhein suggested to the Administrative Officer (AOL Adam that it would be advisable to move the Dinkas out of Dhein immediately for their own safety, because they might be attacked again. These merchants offered to provide transport. However, the AO decided to wait until the next morning, when the security committee was scheduled to meet at 11 lam. This information was given to us by Dr Abdel Rahman al–Zaki, the emissary of the Doctors' Trade Union sent to Dhein after the massacre.

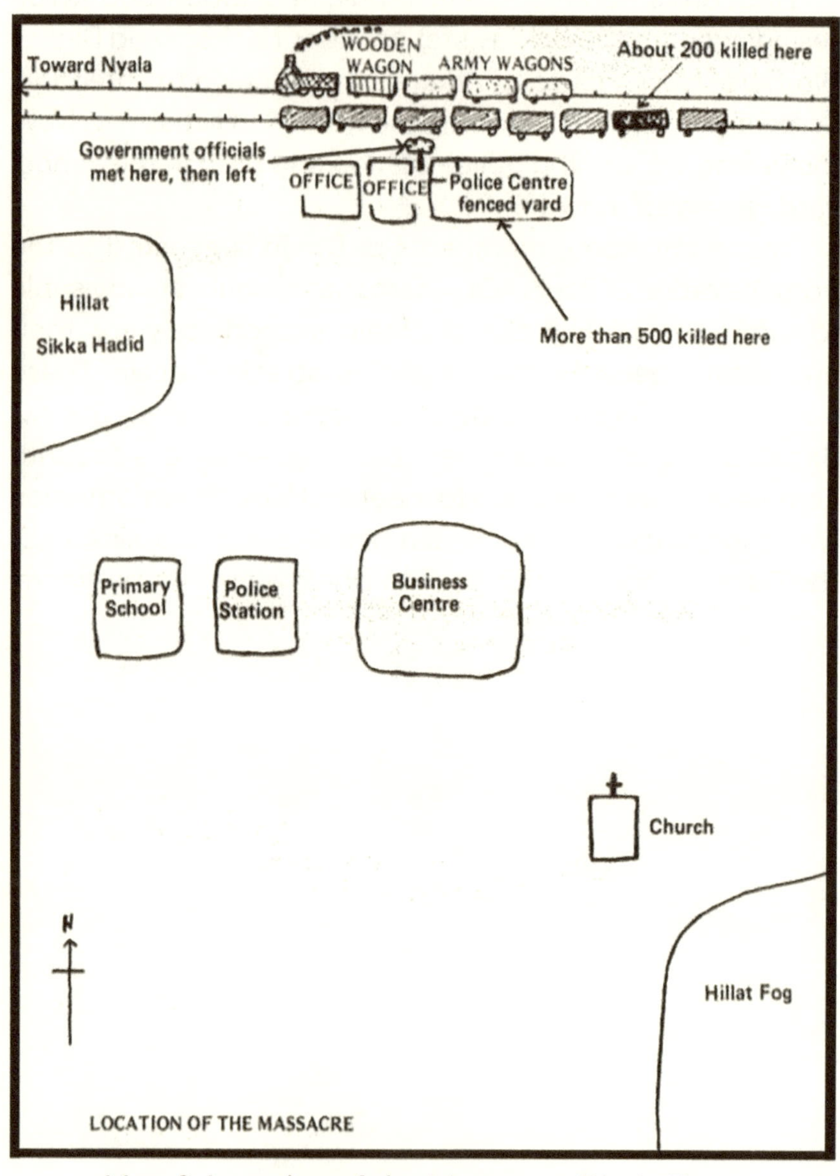

Map 3: Location of the Massacre: Dhein Town

Saturday March 28

Saturday was the day of the massacre. By the evening of that day, more than a thousand Dinka children, women, and men had died — killed by groups of Rizeigat Arabs and other ethnic groups.

The events of this day include: the decision by government officials to move the thousands of Dinkas who spent the night in Hillat Sikka Hadid to the railway station; the attack by the Rizeigat and others on the Dinkas; the meeting of the government officials and the police in the train station to evaluate the situation, and their subsequent withdrawal when the massacre was taking place,' the killing and burning to death of Dinkas in the railway station and in the town; the first train leaving to Nyala ten hours after the beginning of the massacre — carrying the first batch of the survivors.

We will describe each of these events separately.

1. The decision to move the Dinkas to the railway station

At seven a.m. on Saturday March 28, the AO, Adam al-Tahir, accompanied by the deputy chief of police, Ali al-Manna, and another police officer, came to Hillat Sikka Hadid where the Dinkas had spent the night. With the arrival of a goods train at the railway station, these government officials took the decision to move the Dinkas to the station and send them to Nyala. They informed the Dinka chiefs of their decision, and the latter relayed it in Arabic and Dinka to their people, who agreed.

2. The Dinkas distributed to the wagons and the police centre

On arrival at the railway station, the Dinkas moved into eight (or six) wagons. Six (or four) of these were steel wagons similar to containers, and two were open wooden wagons. When these wagons were completely full, several hundred other Dinkas took refuge in the police centre, which is composed of a large room and a 200 square metre fenced yard. Others waited under trees in the railway station.

We should note here that not all wagons were on the same tracks. Seven (or five' wagons, filled with Dinka children, men and women were on the first track. On the track behind was one of the two wooden wagons, just behind the engine. Also attached to this were three wagons with supplies for the army, which were protected by four soldiers.

The distribution of the Dinkas into the wagons and the police centre was completed quietly under police supervision. It was about Barn. As it turned out tater, the railway station was to prove a death trap for more than a thousand Dinkas.

3. News spreads and mobs move into station

As the Dinkas moved into the wagons, news of this spread into the town. Hundreds of Rizeigat and others took to the station. They were determined to stop the Dinkas from leaving Dhein.

The attackers were mainly Rizeigat: but others joined them. There were men and young boys, armed with sticks, spears, knives, swords, axes, and guns — Some Russian made Kalashnikovs. Some were on horseback. One man was pushing a drum of diesel fuel with the help of some young boys.

On their way to the station, the attackers encountered many Dinkas who had spent the night in hiding and were now heading for the station. These were chased. beaten up, and many were killed and burnt to death.

4. Beginnings

The first task of the attackers was to stop the train from leaving. This was effectively accomplished by threatening the train driver and placing blocks of wood on the rails.

Then the attackers began to harass the Dinkas and beat them up. At this time the police were still there. Their actions oscillated between active protection and passivity.

Moreover, the steel wagons provided an effective shelter for the Dinkas who closed them from inside. In addition, some Dinka youths were armed with spears which made a direct attack on the difficult.

In the following sections we will show how the attackers overcame these difficulties, and how police protection came to a sudden end.

5. Government officials meet in the railway station

Many eyewitness survivors confirmed that a meeting was held at about loam under a tree in the railway station white the harassment of the Dinkas was going on. This meeting was attended by the top government official, police officers, and members of the security committee. Also present were two top Rizeigat chiefs, Ali al-Radi and Hammad Bushara, and the four soldiers who were guarding the army wagons.

While the meeting was taking place, some of the attackers confronted the meeting and conducted acts of defiance. They jumped, fired shots in the air, and one asked the participants in the meeting to 'leave the Dinkas to me'.

The meeting suddenly adjourned, and the government officials, including the police, left. The two Rizeigat sheikhs also left.

Now the attackers were left alone with the Dinkas. And the massacre proceeded with full force.

6. How the massacre was conducted

Dozens of eyewitness survivors described the massacre.

The attackers moved onto one of the wooden wagons, which contained more than 200 Dinkas. They threw thatch and burning mattresses into it and burnt all the Dinkas beseiged in it to death.

The attackers also beseiged the police centre where more than 500 Dinkas had taken refuge inside the room and the fenced yard. A Rizeigat man who is known to several of the survivors was active in this attack. He and others brought a drum of diesel fuel and sprinkled the fuel on mattresses, empty sacks, and grass mats, which they lit and continued to throw onto the Dinkas inside. All eyewitness survivors who were on the wagons watching this said that nobody survived in the police centre carnage. The fire burned on the dead bodies until the following day.

Now for the steel wagons. Hundreds of Dinkas closed the six (or four) wagons and stayed inside. The attackers devised specific ways to get at the Dinkas. Many Rizeigat children, women, and men ran to the neighbouring grass huts. They tore them down and brought the grass to the station. This grass was pushed under the steel wagons and set on tire. Burning sacks were also pushed through the ends of the wagon windows. The attackers waited outside.

The Dinkas inside started opening the windows and doors of the wagons to let out the suffocating smoke and the increasing heat. The attackers threw rocks at them and those with guns went on shooting inside the wagons. When some Dinkas left the wagons and tried to escape, they were chased, beaten, killed, and their bodies mutilated and burned.

The attackers also robbed the dead bodies of money and clothes before burning them. One survivor said a Rizeigat woman, whom she identified by name, stabbed her with a knife, stole her money, and snatched her 4 month old baby.

Inside the town, the Dinkas who were hiding or attempting to escape were chased and killed.

Hospital doctors reported that a Dinka patient was dragged from his sick bed and killed. They also reported that a Dinka who was brought to the hospital to be treated for wounds was killed. Hundreds of Rizeigat women stood in front of the hospital and prevented the wounded from approaching it.

Saturday night to Sunday Morning

At about 6pm, the massacre stopped. The Rizeigat left. We received unconfirmed reports that the government officials walked through the streets with loudspeakers asking the Dinkas in hiding to head towards the railway station.

At 7pm the first train started to move towards Nyala. It pulled only one wagon, the wooden one, whose occupants were hardly affected because they were on the track behind the other wagons. Then some small groups of Dinka fled the station into the neighbouring villages. The rest remained in their wagons until Sunday morning when another train came from Babanusa and took them to Nyala.

How many died?

Several figures were given by various sources: the chief doctor of Dhein Hospital, the Minister of the Interior, the Governor of Bahr el-Ghazal Province, an unidentified government official in Dhein, and the Islamic Front Partw We will discuss the figures given by each of these sources and then indicate why we talk in this report about more than a thousand dead'.

First: The Dhein Hospital Story:

After the massacre, the Doctors' Trade Union sent a two doctor delegation to Dhein to assist the hospital staff and to report on what had happened. Dr Abdel Rahman al-Zaki informed us on his return that the chief doctor in Dhein. Dr. Bashar, had told them that the dead who were buried by the health authorities in two mass graves near the railway station numbered 212.

This figure of 212 dead is apparently reliable since it comes from Dr Bashar, himself from Dhein However, we have amassed enough information to refute this figure. And we have no reservations about stating that Dr. Bashar's figure, which was given to the Doctors' Trade Union, is false.

Second: The Government's Version:

On June 20, 1987, the Minister of the Interior, Sid Ahmed al-Hussein was making a speech before the Parliament about security in the Sudan. When asked by an MP from Southern Kordofan about the Dhein massacre, the Minister had the following to say: "The total number of those killed in the Dhein incidents was not more than 183. Then he went on to say that "the number of citizens killed by the rebels in Sataha was very very high".

Four days earlier, the Governor of Bahr el-Ghazal Province, William Ajal Deng, himself a Dinka, told Al-Ayyam newspaper that "the dead did not number more than 300" (Al Ayyam June 14, 1987). Indeed, the Governor, who is a former lawyer, continued to maintain that the massacre was caused by the rebels attacking the Rizeigat in Safaha, a village more than 1 2 hours by road south of Dhein. The Governor also warned people against talking about the massacre in order to make political gains!

On June 24, 1987 Al-Avvam reported in its front page that "an official of Dhein," not identified by name, said the dead numbered not more than fourteen".

Third: Versions given by' the Islamic Front:

The Islamic Front reported three different figures in one week in its news paper, Al-Raya.

On May 6, Al-Raya published a report by Ahmed al-Radi Jabir. He is a distinguished member of the Islamic Front and holds a seat in Parliament. Jabir reported that the dead numbered more than 900. He even gave details: "More than 400 in the railway station. Nearly 200 around the water yard. And 300 in the church".

Four days later, on May 10. Al-Raya published an investigative report entitled The Events of Dhein. In this report it was stated that "the angry Rizeigat attacked the railway station and killed 367 Dinkas whom they found inside".

On the same day, May 10, the Islamic Front held a press conference and stated the following in a report distributed to the participants:

> "There are no exact statistics about the dead. However, the number of those actually buried was 426 Dinkas and 10 Rizeigat."

The Islamic Front did not say how it came by these exact figures.

Fourth: More than a thousand dead:

While investigating the massacre, we were particularly interested to discover the number of the dead. We have collected information which indicates that more than a thousand people died:

1. All eyewitnesses interviewed confirmed that the police centre was completely full with children, women, and men. Policeman Dhieu Bak Dhieu, an eyewitness survivor, told us that at least 500 people were in the 200 square metre fenced yard and the police post. Of these there were about 37 railway labourers from the Jur ethnic group. Eyewitnesses confirmed that all the people here were burnt to death and that there were no survivors.
2. The eyewitnesses confirmed that one wooden wagon, full of Dinkas, was burnt to the ground. There were no survivors here either.
3. Many Dinkas who were inside the steel wagons were killed by bullets, and wounds inflicted by swords, spears, knives, and sticks. Some witnesses gave graphic descriptions of the bodies in front of the wagons.
4. An unidentified number of Dinkas was killed in the streets of Dhein, in two bakeries and on brick-making sites. A 12-year•old Rizeigat boy told us that there

were heaps of bodies in the streets: "here five, there ten". Another Rizeigat youth told us that he saw people dragging bodies to the area outside the town.

5. We have asked eyewitness survivors to give us the names of relatives whom they know were killed in the massacre. We have so far collected a list of 315 from only 20 survivors. An assistant is continuing this task in Nyala.

6. The Dinkas in Dhein numbered 16,970 excluding children in May 1986, according to a census conducted by a religious group for the purposes of relief and Islamization. The difference between that figure and the few thousands in Kas 1000) and Nyala (2000) and Khartoum (4000?) leaves us with a number of missing in the thousands.

All the above facts taken together, make the figure of 'more than a thousand dead' still conservative.

The Identity of the murderers

Those who were involved in the massacre are inhabitants of Dhein. The majority of them were Rizeigat, white some from other ethnic groups participated. There were men, women and youths.

The eyewitness survivors provided us with the names of several of those who participated in the massacre. They also gave descriptions of several others, including a policeman who was dressed in a jallabiya.

There were other witnesses, too: the government officials who he'd their meeting in the station when the massacre started. They saw faces of some of the attackers. We give below a list of these witnesses:

1. Adam al-Tahir, the Administrative Officer of the District:
2. Ali al-Manna, the Deputy Police Chief of Dhein;
3. Jamal Abdel-Rahman, Police Officer and Head of the Passport and Nationality Office in Dhein;
4. Abdel-Rahim al-Fideili, Police Officer, his deputy;
5. Adam Sultan, Prison Guard;
6. Chief of the Fire Department:
7. The policeman in charge of security in Dhein;
8. Several policemen who work in the police station, in the railway station, and in the passport department;
9. four soldiers from the Armed Forces;
10. Ali al-Radi, a Rizeigat chief;
11. Hammad Bushara, a Rizeigat chief.

The identity of some of those who participated in the massacre is known, as is that of many of the witnesses.

The role of the police during the massacre

Eyewitness survivors gave details of the behaviour of the police during the massacre. Many reported how the police left when the killing started. Several gave descriptions of a policeman dressed in a jallabiya who participated in the killing. One woman said that this policeman, who had thick hair and was dressed in a jallabiya, shot and killed her uncle. Deng Alwel. Several others gave descriptions of a policeman who demanded £S.5 from each Dinka in the wooden wagon to pav for his protection services. About thirty Dinkas paid him.

Policeman Dhieu Bak Dhieu, a member of the police force in Dhein, gave this inside view about the Deputy Chief of Police, Ali al-Manna:

"He was in shock. He was frightened. His colour changed. His orders were confused. When he came and Saw people lying dead, he was afraid. He left and sat in his office. He abandoned his men."

Dhieu Bak Dhieu said that the Deputy Chief of Police 'Ordered us not to shoot' at the attackers. He said, however, that another police officer, Abdel-Rahman al–Fideili, himself a Rizeigat, shot straight at the attackers in defence of the Dinkas.

The fate of Father Benjamin Kon and the Dinka Chiefs

One of the mysteries of the massacre relates to the circumstances of the death of Reverend Father Benjamin Kon and two Ginka chiefs: Malith Gum and Deng Alwel. Several eyewitnesses said these three were seen several times that Saturday in a police car together with the AO. Adam al–Tahir, and the Deputy Police Chief Ali al–Manna. They made several trips between the station and the town.

However, one eyewitness said a police officer brought their bodies to the station saying they had been killed by the mobs. Yet as we have reported, one female eyewitness claimed that a plain–clothes policeman shot and killed Deng Alwel. The stories are partly contradictory. But Adam al–Tahir and Ali al–Manna may be able to provide information that may shed some light on this mystery.

The massacre was planned

We have received information from the survivors which indicates that the massacre was planned, and that the police knew in advance of a possible attack by the Rizeigat on the Dinka.

Some Dinkas were informed

One of the survivors, Ariek Piol, was approached by a policeman on a personal basis. Piol, who is one Of the leaders of the Dinka in Dhein and a Muslim, said this policeman came to him on Thursday, March 26. He told him of an impending attack on the Dinkas and advised him to ask the Dinkas to leave the town immediately. Ariek Piol told his people. But their response was sceptical. Few believed the story and left Dhein on Friday morning. Indeed, when some Rizeigat saw some Dinkas on lorries leaving the town, they tried to stop them.

The police warned the Dinka leaders

That same Thursday March 26, the police summoned all the Dinka leaders in Dhein and told them to ask their people to be careful. They asked them to tell all their people to stay at home and not congregate in large numbers.

The police force itself was put on alert from Wednesday March 25 to the evening of Friday March 27 — as reported to us by Dhieu Bak Dhieu.

The story of Ago/ Ako/

A survivor, Agol Akol, who is 50 years Old, told us that she overheard some people talking about 'ridding Dhein of Dinkas' only four days before the massacre. She identified three people by name who were present during that conversation. She then told her brother-in-law and others about it. They did not believe her.

The Aftermath

Early on the morning of Sunday, March 29, the first train arrived in Nyala carrying about 200 survivors of the massacre. At 3pm that same day, the second train arrived with Some 800 survivors. 32 wounded — and 2 dead, who had died during the journey from Dhein.

The survivors who left Dhein by train, lorry, or on foot may be found today in Kas, Nyala, Fasher, Tulus, Buram, and Khartoum.

Those in Kas and Nyala have received food and medical assistance from Oxfam, the Red Cross, USAID, EEC, and Sudan Council of Churches. The people of Kas provided some food and shelter. However, the food provided by the different organisations will run out around the first week of July 1987.

After the massacre, dead bodies were strewn over the streets of Dhein and in the railway station. These bodies became bloated and started to decompose. The people of Dhein were afraid that an epidemic would break out in the town. Reports say some bodies were dumped in latrines, some dragged outside the town, and others buried in mass graves north of the railway station and in the town cemetery.

We should finally note that we collected strong evidence that several Dinka children and young girls were kidnapped during the massacre by some Rizeigat Arabs. While investigating this, we came to discover that the enslavement of Dinka children and women has become common in this area in the last few years. A separate report about slavery in the Rizeigat community and the government's connivance in this is under preparation.

Directions for Action

There are five directions for action towards the massacre and its effects:

1. Providing immediate help for the survivors in Kas, Nyala, Khartoum, and other places.
2. Exerting pressure for action to free those Dinka children and women currently enslaved, and to end the institution of slavery in the Sudan.
3. Providing legal assistance for the survivors and the victims' relatives (at least some of the murderers are known by name and location; and there are many witnesses).
4. Continuing the uncovering of all the details of the massacre. Intellectuals from the Rizeigat, the Dinka, and others should work together to prepare a more detailed report, and for further analysis of the causes of the massacre and of inter-ethnic violence in the area.
5. Forming an investigative committee independent of the government.
6. We believe all the above could be embarked upon simultaneously — and immediately.

CHAPTER THREE

ROOTS OF THE MASSACRE

The massacre of Dhein resulted in more than a thousand dead among the Dinka. It also resulted in the kidnapping and enslavement by some Rizeigat Arabs of an unknown number of Dinka children and women.

The sheer magnitude of the carnage in Dhein deserves an explanation that goes beyond the government's cynical rationalisation of the massacre. The Prime Minister, Sadiq al-Mahdi, said on BBC Radio that the killing in Dhein was carried out in revenge for an attack by the SPLA on Safaha, an area One day by lorry south of Dhein. The Minister of the Interior, Sid Ahmad al Hussein, and the Governor of Bahr al-Ghazal William Ajal Deng, gave similar explanations. (BBC Radio May 31. Constituent Assembly proceedings June 20, and Al-Ayyam newspaper June 14, respectively).

The government's explanations are tantamount to a cover-up, and are directed at deflecting attention from the role of government policy in the area in causing the massacre. Indeed, the government's explanation indicates its aversion to bringing to justice the murderers who are known to it by name and who perpetrated the massacre. Neither does the government intend to question the role and behaviour of its officials and the police during the massacre.

The massacre of Dhein cannot be easily explained away as an isolated act triggered by a sudden desire for revenge.

We have shown that it was premeditated, planned, and carefully executed.

The root causes of the massacre are the following: —

First: Government policy towards the Dinka, Misseiriya, and Rizeigat in the area of ethnic interaction around Bahr al-Arab-Kiir, and its strategy in combating the SPLA.

Second: The emergence of armed banditry against the Dinka by the Rizeigat as a means of enrichment. Also in the context of government policy toward the Dinka and the SPLA.

Third: The emergence of slavery as an institution with favourable conditions of reproduction in the context of government policy.

Fourth: The exacerbation of religious and ethnic strife in Dhein, and of interethnic compatition for resources and services.

The government has firmly introduced the Rizeigat ethnic group into its war with the SPLA. This has resulted in a disruption of the Rizeigat community. Armed banditry, involving the killing of Dinka villagers, has become a regular activity for the government-supported Rizeigat militias. Also linked with the armed attacks on Dinka villages are the kidnapping and subsequent enslavement of Dinka children and women. All this is practiced with the full knowledge of the government. Moreover, ethnic chauvinism among the Rizeigat is being fuelled by the social changes related to the migrations of thousands of drought- and war-affected people, the increasingly complex nature of the economy, the inter-ethnic competition over resources and services, local political animosities, class disparities, and generational strife.

The above social forces and phenomena have interacted and generated racist beliefs and hostile attitudes towards the Dinkas in Dhein, whose numbers reached about 20 thousand. The massacre was the bloody materialisation of those beliefs and attitudes. And government policy was at the root of it all.

1. Government policy in the area

In 985, small units of the SPLA started to be seen in the area south of Bahr al Arab Kiir. This was Dinka land. And it was the year of the famine in the North. Several Rizeigat groups came that year and settled with the Dinka, and were given land to cultivate near the villages of Achiro, Marial Bai, Ajok, and others, Dinka–Rizeigat relations had been cordial since the last Conciliation Accord in Babanusa in 1976. Their presence in the Dinka area was not disturbed by the SPLA units.

However, the Transitional Military Council (TMC), which was then ruling the country, devised a comprehensive strategy towards possible developments that might emanate from the SPLA presence in the area. This strategy was based on the understanding that the Dinka in this area constitute the major potential support for the SPLA on the human, material, food, and information levels. It was thought that they would provide critical logistical support in bringing the war to the areas north of Bahr al-Arab-Kiir. Consequently, it became essential, according to this rationale, to seek to undermine Dinka support for the SPLA — in all its forms.

General Burma Nasir, then a member of the TMC, was outspoken in his support of measures towards implementing this strategy, The issue was discussed in the newspapers. And when Sad al-Mahdi became Prime Minister he advocated this strategy in an even more vigorous fashion, albeit couched in intentionally ambiguous language about the need to "appreciate the inter-tribal situation in the area" Indeed, Sadig al-Mahdi appointed General Burma Nasir as State Minister for Defence.

The core of the strategy to undermine SPLA support in the Dinka area was to resurrect and fuel the historical Dinka-Rizeigat strife which was put to rest by the accord of 1976 in Babanusa. Indeed the two groups coexisted relatively peacefully and continued to interact with only minor individual conflicts.

The government's methods of forcing the Rizeigat, and also the Misseiriya to the east, into the war included the arming of the Misseiriya marahil (nomads) who were already armed, with more powerful guns and ammunition, and the establishment among the Rizeigat of armed militias.

This government policy, which we present in Outline only, has resulted in several attacks by the Rizeigat militias and the Misseiriya marahil on the Dinka villages south of Bahr al-Arab-Kiir.

Towards the end of 1985, the Dinka chiefs in Awiel received information about an agreement between the Misseiriya and the Rizeigat to jointly attack the Dinkas south of Bahr al-Arab-Kiir. On December 21, 1985, the first attack took place- Armed groups of the Misseiriya and Rizeigat attacked and killed Dinka officers and soldiers working in the Game, Police, and Prison units at Ariath, 17 miles from Awiel. The Governor of Bahr al-Ghazal at that time was General Albino Akol, himself a Dinka. A small army unit chased away the attackers and returned the cattle stolen during the attack.

On January 12, 1986, large numbers of armed Rizeigat and Misseiriya attacked the Dinka villages of Marial Bai, Nyamlel, Achana and several others. Reports stated that 612 Dinkas were killed, including the son of the Dinka Sultan Riiny. A large number of cattle were taken, dhura (sorghum) was burnt, houses were also burnt down, and more than 700 children and women kid were also burnt down, and more than 700 children and women kidnapped.

Similar attacks continued through February 1986 and after, until the SPLA deployed heavier forces in the area in May - June 1986. It was only then that Dinka villagers could cultivate food, under SPLA protection.

Then a sudden attack by the Rizeigat militias occurred in January 1987. This time the Rizeigat were aided by some Fallata Umbararu. The attack was particularly devastating in Marial Bai, Achiro and neighbouring villages. An unknown number of Dinka villagers, mainly men, were killed. Again food, homes, and property were burnt to the ground. Hundreds of children and women were kidnapped. We will show later that these were taken as slaves.

In February 1987, large numbers of Rizeigat attacked the Dinka villages for more cattle and slaves. This time they did not succeed because they were confronted by SPLA forces. They were defeated with heavy casualties.

In mid March 1987, news reached the army in Nyala that the SPLA had been sighted near Safaha. Army units moved into the area and engaged in fighting with the SPLA There are contradictory reports about this However, it is known that in the following days the SPLA and the Rizeigat militias engaged in several battles. The Rizeigat were defeated with heavy casualties. Then SPLA forces returned south with large numbers of Dinka cattle which had previously been taken by the Rizeigat in their January 1987 attack. These were the Safaha events which the Prime Minister said were the cause of the Dhein massacre.

The government has squarely introduced the Rizeigat (and the Misseiriva) into its war with the SPLA with the intention of undermining potential support for the SPLA in the Dinka area. The results of this policy were mixed as far as government objectives are concerned. Large numbers of Dinkas were killed, or kidnapped for enslavement. Their cattle wealth was destroyed. Their lives were completely disrupted. Thousands migrated north to Dhein, Nyala, Khartoum, and other towns. However, thousands joined the SPLA. And these were said to be the ones who attacked Safaha to get back their stolen cattle.

Such were the results of government policy at one level. At another level, this policy created certain distortions in the social structure and life of the Rizeigat community. The distortions are related to the emergence of armed and criminal banditry as a quick means of gaining wealth from the sale Of Dinka cattle; and to the return of slavery as an institution. These developments interacted with the upsurge of ethnic chauvinism in the Rizelgat community to generate an insidious psychic structure that made the massacre possible.

2. Armed banditry against the Dinka

The government policy to support the arming of Rizeigat militias has resulted in these militias conducting regular raids on Dinka villages to kill men, rob cattle and property, and to kidnap children and women. Cattle robbery has become a quick means of enrichment.

Several Dinkas have told us that the bulk of their cattle have been stolen by the Misseiriya and Rizeigat. They also gave us specific information relating to the involvement of government officials in the sale of their stolen cattle.

The stolen cattle have become a continual issue of contention between the Dinkas and the Rizeigat in Safaha, Dhein, and in the villages in the area. There were newspaper reports of this strife in Khartoum itself. Some cases were taken to court. The stolen cattle were the focus of conflicts, fights and complaints. Several Dinkas tried to take back their cattle seen in Dhein. Stolen cattle were also the reason why the SPLA attacked Safaha, to get them back.

There are other cases of banditry not related to cattle which were also perpetrated by the armed militias. The perpetrators are known by name to some of the victims and their relatives Some eyewitnesses have provided us with the names of the militias' members in Safaha. And they told us of their involvement in a gruesome attack on a lorry owned by a Dinka just outside Safaha. They provided us with the names of 30 Dinkas who were killed in that attack. This was in 1986. The burnt-out lorry is stationed in the Dhein police station today. No one was brought to justice.

Majok Jieng Majok witnessed the attack by the Rizeigat militias on his village, Marial Bai, in February 1987. And he described their banditry.

> "These Rizeigat, when they came in February,
> they took our sugar. They took the clothes of
> women. They took every good piece of cloth,
> and everything that was good. Mattresses, this
> they took. I have seen all this. They took my

shirt. They took everything. Even the cups with which we drink water, they took."

Armed banditry is a new distortion in Rizeigat society. It was created by the government policy of arming militias and Of not preventing them from attacking Dinka villages — not to mention cynical encouragement. The linkage between armed banditry and the Dhein massacre is that beliefs have been generated in the Rizeigat consciousness that Dinka property and life are fair game and that there is no fear of government or legal intervention.

3. Slavery in the Rizeigat Community

Slavery is another distortion in Rizeigat society. In the past there were individual and isolated cases of slavery that were disguised and rationalised as kinship. However, since 1986 slavery has returned in force, and is not seen by the perpetrators as illegitimate in the context Of the present government war policy. The kidnapping of Dinka children, young girls, and women, their subsequent enslavement, their use in the Rizeigat economy and other spheres of life, and their exchange for money — all these are facts. And the government has full knowledge of them. Indeed, the perpetrators of kidnapping and slavery are its allies in the armed militias.

The reason why we are mentioning slavery in this report about the massacre is that some Dinka children and young girls were kidnapped during the massacre and are currently being held by some Rizeigat families in Dhein. Moreover, the existence of slavery in the area has generated beliefs among the Rizeigat that the Dinka is subhuman. All psychological barriers to terminating his existence have been broken down. That was what made the massacre in Dhein possible — without fear of reprisals by the government whose representatives were present.

While we were investigating the massacre, some of the survivors told us that information has reached them that their children held by the Rizeigat in Dhein are currently being sold, and that there are hundreds (some said thousands) of Dinka children and women enslaved by Rizeigat families in villages and towns whose names they provided. They gave us many names of relatives currently living in slavery. And some gave the names of the individuals holding them as slaves. They also told us that they have complained to government officials and to the police to no avail.

So we decided to start an investigation into slavery in the area, and we now feel we have confirmed reports that slavery exists. We are convinced that it is not anything else but slavery in its classical sense.

Below we give a very brief summary of the testimonies of witnesses, relatives and former slaves — newly liberated. We do this to argue that slavery is directly and indirectly connected to the Dhein massacre. We give the details of the testimonies about slavery in a separate chapter at the end of the report.

> *First*: Eyewitness survivor Nyaniok Dut Anai provided us with information about some Dinka children and women held by the Rizeigat in Dhein. She saw these children and women while she was looking for her children lost during the massacre. She talked to some of them and they gave the names of their villages and chiefs. Some of the women whom she met were captured before the massacre in the Dinka villages south of Bahr al-Arab-Kiir.

Second: James Deng Anyuon, a Dinka who now lives in Nyala, talked to us about slavery in Darfur. He even gave the name of his brother, now dead, who was sold for ten camels in Um Jidad. And he gave information relating to the role of Al-Fashir police in handing the runaway slave back to his relative.

Third: Policeman Dhieu Bak Dhieu, a Dinka who worked in Dhein and survived the massacre, told us of a specific case of Dinka woman coming to the Dhein police asking for her child to be returned from the family which had taken him as slave.

Fourth: Majok Jieng Majok provided us with strong evidence of the existence of slavery. He has been very active in helping the slaves to escape. Indeed we met and interviewed two of the ex-slaves whom he had helped. And Majok gave a list of some slaves still held by known Rizeigat and another list of ex-slaves whom he sent to Dinka relatives in Khartoum. Maiok also told us about the treatment and uses of enslaved Dinkas.

Fifth: We had long recorded interviews with two Dinka ex-slaves: twelve-year-old Abuk Diing and 30-year-old Abuk Thiep. They talked about their capture in Mabior Nyang and Achoro, the trip on foot north, their allocation to the captors, arrival in the captors' village, the work they used to do, and how they escaped.

We believe the government policy of arming Rizeigat militias and sending them into Dinka areas has created favourable conditions for the re-emergence of slavery. Today new economic needs are felt among some factions ot the Rizeigat for slave labour.

And in the context of government connivance, racist attitudes among the Rizeigat are generated against the Dinkas It was these attitudes which made the massacre possible, and justifiable in their eyes.

4. Social Conflict in Dhein Society

When the massacre occurred. Dhein was not a quiet, peaceful, or harmonious town. Its society was impregnated with the forces and elements of the massacre. Religious fanaticism was on the rise. Competition over resources and services started to be played along ethnic lines. A new Rizeigat ethnic identity was being moblised against other ethnicities. Thuggery and disdain for convention and law became common among the Rizeigat youth. The social fabric of the Rizeigat community started to disintegrate. There was a generational conflict between the old and the young, and class conflict between the haves and the have nots — these mainly young. And there were also political divisions.

These conflicts interacted with ethnic violence, armed banditry, and slavery to generate the psychosis necessary for the massacre.

The church in Dhein was the focus of religious fanaticism, competition over land, and irrational suspicion. In 1986, some four hundred Dhein Moslems signed a petition to the judge asking for the removal of the church from the town. Sometime later, the church was involved in a dispute with some Rizeigat families who built their homes on church land.

The court ruled in favour of the church, and this created bitterness among the Rizeigat families.

Catechist James Deng Achol told us of an unannounced visit by a police officer to the church. He had come to ask about the 'devices' on top of the church, and about the source Of the strong light that did not make any noise like normal generators. The officer was referring to the silicon panels used by the church to collect solar energy for light. Also, we have referred to the meeting called for by the police with the Dinka chiefs on the eve of the massacre. We mentioned that a police officer, Jamal Abdel–Rahman, asked Father Benjamin Kon about all the 'meetings' held by the church every Sunday.

Dhein was also experiencing competition and conflict over services like water and the grinding of dhura. Several Dinkas told us about their children and women being beaten up, verbally abused, pushed from the line, and their water containers snatched and destroyed. They said their complaints to the police only brought them further abuse from the police. They were advised to leave Dhein since they were not liked there.

Marek Deng, a handicapped youth who uses sticks to walk, told us of the verbal slurs hurled at him by men, women, and children — epithets like jangawi (a perjorative term for Dinka) and abid (slave).

Some factions of the Rizeigat also started to agitate and mobilise around a Rizeigat ethnicity against the Dinka and the Zaghawa. Some time before the massacre, a number of Rizeigat youth gathered in the market place with the intention Of attacking the Zaghawa merchants. They said these merchants were hiking up prices. In the process, the car of a Zaghawa chief was destroyed. In another incident, some Rizeigat youth destroyed some kiosks that had been given to the Zaghawa by the local authorities. We have been told that the Zaghawa in Dheih are arming themselves to ward off any attack by the Rizeigat.

Another example of the Rizeigats' rising sense of ethnicity was symbolic. Some youth tore down the sign carrying the name of the District Council "Majlis Rifi al-Mantiga al-Shargiva" (Eastern District Rural Council). They installed instead another sign which read "Riasat Majlis Dar Rizeigat al-Dhein" (Headquarters 01 the Council of Rizeigat Land in Dhein).

There are conflicts within the Rizeigat community. The old sheikhs and the youth are in disagreement over many issues. The majority of the sheikhs are against the armed attacks On Dinka villages. Some sheikhs are agitating for the reinstating of the idara ahliva (administration by the tribal leaders).

Class differences are rising sharply in Dhein. Many of the youth are unemployed and poor. Their poverty is increasing within the context of the rising enrichment of certain factions from the boom in commerce, agricultural schemes, and cattle wealth. These are the youth for whom the government policy in the area has provided the possibility of enrichment from armed banditry and slavery.

Dhein society was ridden with contradictions and conflict. It was ready to explode at any time and under any pretext. The government has introduced the Rizeigat into its war against the SPLA, which resulted in the distortions of banditry, slavery, and inter-ethnic animosity.

All these distortions and forces interacted to generate a psychosis that defeated the rational part of the Rizeigat community. Thus, the massacre was no more than a bloody picnic.

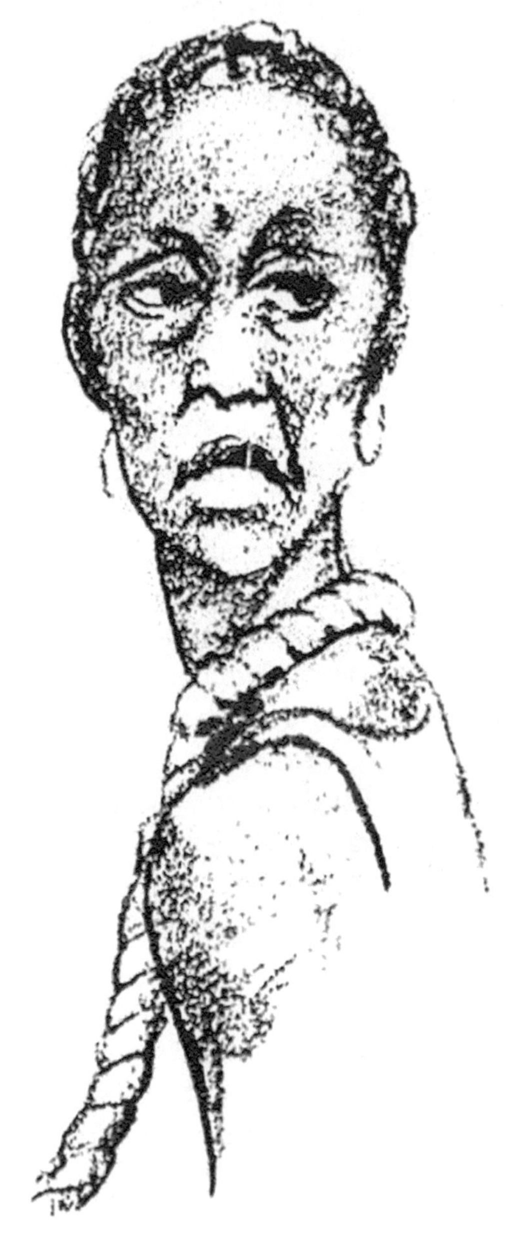

CHAPTER FOUR

SLAVERY IN THE SUDAN..AGAIN

In May–June 1987 we were investigating the Dhein massacre. While interviewing the survivors, they told us about the existence of slavery in the area and we decided to investigate that, too. Thus far we have received information and strong evidence that slavery, in its classical and known sense, has re-emerged in the Sudan.

In the following section, we present extracts from recorded interviews with Dinka men, women, and a child. These persons had been affected by slavery in different ways: one woman had seen children and women enslaved in Dhein, and her own infant was kidnapped during the massacre. A policeman reports of a Dinka woman who came to the police station in Dhein complaining that her son had been enslaved by a particular person. A Dinka man has made it his duty to free Dinkas from slavery. Another man tells of the sale of his brother. An old woman tells how the Rizeigat and another tribe attacked her village and kidnapped 11 of her relatives. And finally, a 12-year-old girl and a young woman tell about their days of slavery.

1. Nyanjok (Tijok) Dut Anai

Nyaniok Dut Anai is a 30-year-old woman. Her husband was killed in the massacre on Saturday March 28, 1987. She was stabbed and knocked unconscious. Her infant was snatched by a Rizeigat woman, and she does not know the whereabouts of her other four children. When we met her in Dhein in early June, she was going from one house to another asking to see the Dinka children hidden in case one of hers was among them.

> My children are five: Emilio, Musulina, Maria Rek, Aduong and Abuk the infant. They took them all.

We asked Nyanjok (Tijok) about how she searches for her children:

> Some Arabs would say to me: "Nyanjok, go to that house. There are Dinka children there". I went. But didn't find my children. So I would go back and return the next day to search. Everyone I meet in the street. I tell him: "Brother, I have lost my children". He tells me: "Such and such has Dinka children in his house". I went. But didn't find my children. Those children I found were very small. So I stay and look.

Nyanjok told us that some Rizeigat Arabs are hiding an unknown number of Dinka children and young women, and that some of these had been kidnapped and enslaved before the massacre. Others were kidnapped during the massacre.

We asked Nyanjok to give us more details about these Dinka children and women, such as descriptions and locations. She said:

I found a girl in a house near the water yard (Donki Sakina). She was seven years old. I also found a grown-up woman who was captured in the war. I asked her about her family. She said their Sultan is called Abd el Bagi Ayii. There are One small and one said she had a husband.

Then I found a small boy in another house. And then another small boy which had been hit on the head. This was near the market. I found a third boy whose ethnic group I know. He is from the people of Sultan Arop. I found these three. This third, they gave him to me and I sent him to his relatives.

Then I found a young woman from my village. And then another girl in a house near Donki Jinubo (Jinubo water yard). These were held by the Arabs.

Then there is another grown-up girl. This one I asked whether she was kidnapped from the railway station during the massacre. She said she was kidnapped from Marial Bai. The area of Sultan Riiny.

Then we asked Tijok whether this last girl was forcefully taken from Marial Bai. She was surprised at our question:

Of course they kidnap people whenever they go to the South, that's why we ran away. Because the South is destroyed. That's why we came here.

2. Dhieu Bak Dhieu

Dhieu Bak Dhieu is a Dinka policeman who survived the massacre in Dhein. He was disarmed by his superiors during the massacre. He was then transferred to Nyala. He had this to Say about kidnapped Dinka children:

> There are Dinka people who sometimes find their own children with some Rizeigat. When they come to the police for help in getting back their children, the police send them away to bring an arida (a court injunction).
>
> I once witnessed a Dinka woman who came to the police station. I was there. She said: "I have found my son with someone. They had taken him from me; and then they dug a hole. They wanted to kill me and bury me in that hole. I escaped, and the man took my son. I came to you to bring my' child back to me." The people in charge at the police station told her to go and bring an arida.

Dhieu Bak Dhieu said the order to 'go and bring an arida' was just a way of not doing anything, since these simple and illiterate people wouldn't know how to get an arida.

3. James Deng Anyuon

James Deng Anyuon is about 45 years old. He lives in Nyala. He used to live in Dhein; but he left it 6 months before the massacre with some few hundred Dinkas. They left because they felt that at that time Dhein was unsafe for Dinkas. They had gone to the Dhein police to complain about attacks by the Rizeigat against their families in the water yard. The police asked them why they were staying in Dhein since the people did not like them anyway. So they left Dhein. He said:

> These Rizeigat attack us. When one of us stands up to protect his cattle, they kill him. Then they take women and girls.
>
> Today there are many Dinka girls in Matarig. Lungara. Farhabil, and Gimelaya. There are others in neighbouring countries. Our sons and daughters. The government is there. But no one pays attention. In June 1986 they brought many. They brought many girls. Like that one I just told you about.
>
> We are citizens. But when we see this we feel we are not Sudanese. Something like this happening by force, when it is brought in front of the government, nobody pays attention.
>
> Today the Rizeigat kidnap women and children and sell them to others.

We asked James for evidence about the sale Of Dinka boys and women:

> Your son was with the Rizeigat. And people saw him there. Then when you meet the man who took him, you say to him •that day, you took my son.' And he says 'No, I did not take him.'

Then James continues:

> My brother, on my father's side, is called Tong Marong. He was kidnapped and taken to Um Jidad. He was sold for 10 camels. He was fifteen. This boy took a camel and ran for two days to Al-Fashir where he complained to the police. From the police station, he was taken to the army barracks to a Dinka relative called Garang Maling 801. This Garang is now in the Army here in Nyala and lives in Hay Buluk.

4. Majok Jieng Majok

Majok Jieng Majok is 35 years Old. He used to live in Abu Matarig, a small town south of Dhein. He had to leave for Nyala when Some Rizeigat Arabs burnt down his house and wanted to kill him. This was because they knew what Majok was doing: helping enslaved Dinkas to escape.

Majok gave us information about enslaved Dinkas in several villages: their names, the names of their captors, and the kind of treatment they receive. Majok directed us to meet a girl and a woman whom he had helped after they escaped and sent to Khartoum. These were Abuk Diing and Abuk Thiep whose stories we present at the end of this report.

Maiok Jieng Majok told us that about 700 Dinka children and women were kidnapped and enslaved by Rizeigat Arabs in June 1986. He said he was then in Abu Matarig, and that he complained about this to Umda Fadl chief of Abu Matarig. The Rizeigat chief, who has good relations with the Dinka and is sympathetic, told Majok that "there is no government that could free these people and return them to their families". Complaints to the police produced a similar response.

Then Majok decided to work to free his people who were scattered in villages like Kiryok, Farhabil. Gimeilaya and other places. He said there are between two hundred and three hundred Dinkas enslaved in Farhabil alone.

We asked Maiok about the services carried out by these enslaved Dinkas:

> They make the girls their women. Like that woman I told you about earlier who is called Madok Auei. This woman is now the 'woman' of Musa Biyetu. Another woman, Man-Nyibol Akol, has become the 'woman' of Gor Hamoda. All this has happened. And I have seen it all with my own eyes.

Majok told us that this Musa Biyetu, a Rizeigi, has another Dinka girl called Anger Malou whom he uses as 'awin bitau' (his 'woman').

What about the children? We asked.

> There are many many children. Some are three years old. These were brought to be wasted. To become their slaves only. To become their servants.

Majok gave us the names of some of the enslaved Dinkas whom he had helped to free. He said there was a girl enslaved by Muhammed Shumi, a Rizeigi. And that he went to a great deal of trouble trying to free her. He succeeded thanks to the help of Umda Fadl al-Nabi, the Rizeigat Sheikh. He sent this girl to a relative of hers in Khartoum called Akol Kwel who is a merchant.

Majok said he also freed the following from slavery and sent them to their relatives: Athieng Dut Ngor, Abuk Gulu Dut, Abuk Akot, Aliang Anai Ngor, Abuk Garang Ngor, Deng Garang Yel, and Abungdit Bak.

When we were in Nyala, Majok showed us two other women whom he said he had freed from slavery. But it was not possible to hold a recorded interview with them then. So Majok directed us to Abuk Diing and Abuk Thiep in Khartoum. And we present their story at the end of this report.

Majok gave more details about the treatment of enslaved Dinkas:

> During cultivation time, the grown-up Dinka is sent to the farm to cut the weeds from morning to evening. And if a Rizeigi has a son, he will not send him for errands any more. Only the Dinka child is sent to do these things. Old Dinka women are made to work in the house and on the farm. They wash the dishes and do many household chores.
>
> These enslaved Dinkas are given nothing. If they are bare-footed, they remain so.
>
> The Dinka girls who are grown-up are made their 'women'. And the girl who is brought young and a virgin is also made a 'woman'.

Majok said he used to contact these enslaved Dinkas and help them to escape. In this, he was assisted by Rizeigat with whom he had sworn a 'brotherhood oath'. This was done when the Rizeigat were his guests in his village, Marial Bai, in 1985 during the drought north Of Bahr al-Arab-Kiir.

5. Alwel Bol Ater

Alwel BOI Ater is a 60 year Old woman. She is from the village of Achiro. Her husband, Macham Macham Angui, was one of the richest Dinkas in the area. He had wealth, cattle, and several wives. The Rizeigat and another group not known exactly to Alwel attacked Achiro in January 1987. They killed Alwel's husband and kidnapped eleven persons from her family. Alwel listed these relatives who were kidnapped whom she has never heard from since:

1. Abuk Macham, Alwel's daughter, married to Deng Aguot, a farmer in Awiel
2. Mangar Deng, Abuk's son, two years old
3. Abuk Adut Macham, 13 years old
4. Majok Macham, 5 years old
5. Zahra Malwal Achot
6. Aboba Malwal Achot
7. Aboba
8. Abuk Du Pieng
9. Abuk Baak Baak Angui
10. Nyanjok Macham
11. Achol Macham

Alwel said the attackers came early in the morning. They were armed, and were riding horses, camels, and donkeys. They burnt the houses to the ground and set fire to the grain in the stores and on the farms. The fire burnt for 8 days, said Alwet. They took all the cattle in addition to killing and kidnapping. She managed to escape to Awiel and eventually came to Khartoum where she is staying with her Son.

Alwel said the Rizeigat are doing all this so that the "Dinka become finished. Then the Rizeigat would take Over this land, Come with their cattle to graze here, and with their families to live".

6. Abuk Thiep and Abuk Diing

Abuk Thiep is 30 years old. Abuk Diing is twelve. The first is from Achiro and the second from Mabior Nyang. We were directed to see them in Khartoum by Majok Jieng Majok. He told us in Nyala that he had sent them to relatives in Khartoum after they had escaped from slavery in a village south of Abu Matarig. We interviewed both in Khartoum through an interpreter. And they told us the following.

In January 1987, some armed Rizeigat attacked the village of Abuk Diing (Mabior Nyang) and the village of Abuk Thiep (Achiro). Twelve-year-old Abuk Diing said the attackers came early in the morning. They killed her father. Then she ran away with her mother Ayuen Anai, and her brothers: Manywal (4 years), Bol (8 years), and Garang (her twin). Abuk was carrying her infant brother (a fifth) as she was running. Her mother was running behind her. The mother took the infant from Abuk, and ordered her to run faster. However, the attackers caught up with Abuk and her brothers. Abuk said she had heard later that her mother and the infant brother escaped and are safe in Mabior Nyang, guarded by the SPLA.

After the attack, the killing, and the kidnapping were over, the attackers divided into small groups each with its own booty. The group which kidnapped Abuk Diing and Abuk Thiep consisted of the following five:

1. Muhammed Buru, the head of the group and the oldest
2. Adam Buru, his young brother
3. Ibrahim
4. Muhammed
5. Anai.

They were armed with one kalany (Kalashnikov rifle), a second gun abu ashara (government-issue .303 rifle), spears, and swords. Each was riding a horse. They had with them a number of cattle. Abuk Thiep said she recognised the cattle as belonging to Umda (Chief) Anai Akok from the village of Wut Giir, Bak Maker from Achiro and Yiil Akok from Ajok.

When the group of five Rizeigat moved towards Safaha, north of Bahr al–Arab–Kiir, they had with them the following Dinka women and children:

1. Abuk Thiep, 30 years, from Achiro
2. Abuk Diing, 12 years, from Mabior Nyang
3. Abungdit Thiik, middle age, from Nyiin Achol
4. Abuk Ding Malwal, 12 years, Achiro
5. Nyanjok Akot, 12 years, Achiro
6. Deng Abik, 4 years, Mabior Nyang. Mother killed
7. Ayuen Aleu, 3 years, Mabior Nyang
8. Ayuen Aleu, 5 years. Mabior Nyang
9. Nyanjok Abik. 12 years, Mabior Nyang
10. Abik Abik, 2 years, Mabior Nyang
11. Nyibol Akot, 3 years, daughter of Abuk Thiep, no. 1.

Abuk Thiep said the journey to Safaha took two days. One Dinka woman to escape along the way. Then the women were tied with a rope round necks. The rope was tied to a horse. The children were carried on the horses.

On the way to Safaha, they met another Rizeigat contingent with a number of Dinka children and women. Abuk Diing said she then saw her 4 year old brother, Manywal, on the back of a horse behind a Rizeigat man among this new group she said she took her brother down from the horse's back. When asked she explained he was her brother. They allowed her to take him. But in Safaha, the Rizeigat man who had kidnapped Manywal came and took him from Abuk. She never saw Manywal again, nor either of her two other brothers.

In a place north of Safaha, the attackers all assembled. It was here that they divided up the booty of cattle, women, and children among themselves. When the cattle were divided, each Rizeigat man got only one. Then came the division of children and women. Each man would come and select his choice. The result of the division was as follows, as far as the group of 5 was concerned:

1. Abuk Thiek and her daughter Nyibol, for Muhammed Buru, the group leader
2. Abuk Diing the 12-year old girl. for Adam Buru
3. Awok Aleu, for Ibrahim
4. Deng Abik and Abuk Diing Malwal, for Muhammed
5. Abungdit Thiek, for Anai.

The rest were distributed to other Rizeigat unknown to Abuk and Abuk.

The group of 5 led by Muhammed Buru headed north with the Dinka women and children and 5 cows. They arrived in the village of the Burus.

The Buru home was a Farig (cattle camp) made of grass huts. The family consisted of the following, listed to us by the 12 year old Abuk Diing:

Buru — the father of Muhammed and Adam. An old man with a white beard
Bab — his wife and mother of the two sons
Mariam — daughter Of Muhammed Buru
Baya and Kunama — two young relatives whose father was absent in Safaha
Hukuma — a 4-year old boy
Ibrahim — a young boy
Two women
Muhammed Buru
Adam Buru

The wife of Muhammed Buru was not present. But after hearing of his return she arrived at the farig, stayed one night and left. Adam was not married.

Abuk Diing and Abuk Thiek talked to us about their 40 days in slavery before they escaped. Abuk Diing the 12-year old, used to take care of the calf when the Burus were milking their only Cow. (They sold the 5 cows robbed from the Dinkas). However, the basic work of the young Abuk was to go every day to the farm, cut the water melons, collect them in heaps, break them open, and extract the seeds. Then she dried the seeds and packed them into sacks.

Abuk Thiek's work included grinding grain into flour and packing it in sacks for storage. She also used to grind okra and sesame.

Abuk Thiek said she was repeatedly beaten by the old Buru whenever the women complained to him about her laxity and bad work.

She also said they were given only flour to make porridge for their food, together with tea leaves and no sugar. She described the Buru diet as composed of flour porridge, dried tomatoes cooked with sesame and beans, and sometimes meat.

Abuk Diing and Abuk Thiek stayed about 40 days in slavery before they decided to run away. The two Buru sons, Muhammed and Adam, had returned south for more kidnapping. However, they did not return on time. And their family seem to have thought that something had happened to them.

Abuk and Abuk escaped one night and reached Abu Matarig after a 10-hour journey on foot. They met Majok Jieng Majok. He took them with him to Nyala and sent them to Khartoum. They are now living with relatives in Khartoum.

These were the personal testimonies of seven Dinka men, women and a child about slavery in Darfur.